EDGE BOOKS™

DINOSAUR WARS

SPINOSAURUS

★★★★★★★★★★

VS.

GIGANOTOSAURUS

★★★★★★★★★★

BATTLE OF THE GIANTS

by Michael O'Hearn

Consultant:
Mathew J. Wedel, PhD
Paleontologist and Assistant Professor
Western University of Health Sciences
Pomona, California

CAPSTONE PRESS
a capstone imprint

Edge Books are published by Capstone Press,
151 Good Counsel Drive, P.O. Box 669, Mankato, Minnesota 56002.
www.capstonepress.com

092009
005619WZS10

Books published by Capstone Press are manufactured with paper
containing at least 10 percent post-consumer waste.

Library of Congress Cataloging-in-Publication Data
O'Hearn, Michael, 1972–
    Spinosaurus vs. Giganotosaurus: battle of the giants / by Michael O'Hearn.
    p. cm. — (Edge books. Dinosaur wars)
    Summary: "Describes the features of Spinosaurus and Giganotosaurus,
and how they may have battled each other in prehistoric times" — Provided
by publisher.
    Includes bibliographical references and index.
    ISBN 978-1-4296-3936-1 (lib. bdg.)
    1. Spinosaurus — Juvenile literature. 2. Giganotosaurus — Juvenile
literature. I. Title.
QE862.S3O345 2010
567.912 — dc22   2009028144

Editorial Credits
Aaron Sautter, editor; Kyle Grenz, designer; Marcie Spence, media researcher;
    Nathan Gassman, art director; Laura Manthe, production specialist

Illustrations
Philip Renne, Jon Hughes, and James Field

Photo Credits
Brett Booth, 6 (left), 18–19 (bottom)
Photo Researchers, Inc/Joe Tucciarone/Science Photo Library, cover (top)
Shutterstock/Leigh Prather, stylized backgrounds
Shutterstock/Steve Cukrov, 18 (top)
Shutterstock/Valery Potapova, parchment backgrounds

TABLE OF
CONTENTS

WELCOME TO DINOSAUR WARS!

Dinosaurs were brutal creatures. They fought each other and ate each other. Usually it was meat-eater versus plant-eater or big versus small. But in Dinosaur Wars, it's a free for all. Plant-eaters attack plant-eaters. Giants fight giants. And small dinosaurs gang up on huge opponents. In Dinosaur Wars, any dinosaur battle is possible!

In this dinosaur war, Spinosaurus and Giganotosaurus battle to the death. You will see how these massive meat-eaters match up. You'll learn about their giant weapons and how they used them in combat. Then you'll see them battling head-to-head — and you'll get to watch from a front row seat!

Spinosaurus (SPINE-uh-sore-uhs)
Giganotosaurus (jee-gah-NOTE-uh-sore-uhs)

THE COMBATANTS

SPINOSAURUS VS. GIGANOTOSAURUS

Spinosaurus and Giganotosaurus never actually fought. Spinosaurus lived on the northern coast of Africa. Meanwhile, Giganotosaurus lived at the southern tip of South America.

Still, before they became **extinct**, they did share the earth for 15 million years. Giganotosaurus survived for 32 million years, from 122 to 90 million years ago. Spinosaurus lived about half as long, from 110 to 95 million years ago.

These were two of the largest **predators** ever to walk the earth. They probably wouldn't have hunted each other. However, if they had lived in the same area, they may have fought over a meal. After all, they were both so big that they had to eat a lot of food.

Tyrannosaurus rex was once thought to be the largest land predator ever. But both Spinosaurus and Giganotosaurus were longer and heavier than T. rex. They were the largest land predators of all time.

FIERCE FACT
BIGGEST PREDATORS

extinct — no longer living anywhere in the world

predator — an animal that hunts other animals for food

SIZE

Spinosaurus was about 55 feet (17 meters) long from head to tail. That's more than the width of a basketball court. Spinosaurus' head measured almost 6 feet (1.8 meters) long. He had a spiny sail on his back, similar to the back fins of many fish. The sail stood more than 6 feet (1.8 meters) high at the tallest point. Spinosaurus weighed more than 9 tons (8.2 metric tons). He had the size and strength to overpower almost anything that got in his way.

Spinosaurus' sail was likely used to identify others of its own kind. It may have also made him look larger than he really was to scare off other dinosaurs.

Giganotosaurus was one of the few creatures in history that could match Spinosaurus in size. At 50 feet (15 meters) long, Giganotosaurus was a little shorter than Spinosaurus. But what Giganotosaurus lacked in length, he made up for in weight. He tipped the scales at about 8.5 tons (7.7 metric tons.) Although he was slightly smaller than Spinosaurus, Giganotosaurus would still be tough to take down in a fight.

SPEED AND AGILITY

Spinosaurus
Sleek and quick
★ ★ ★

★ ★
Giganotosaurus
Stocky and powerful

Giganotosaurus had strong back legs and probably ran fast for short distances. But with his stockier frame, he likely couldn't stop or turn quickly. Giganotosaurus probably hunted giant long-necked dinosaurs that didn't move quickly. He didn't need to be fast to be a successful hunter.

Spinosaurus was sleeker and more streamlined than the stocky Giganotosaurus. He could probably move quickly on land. But Spinosaurus had a bigger advantage in the water, where he hunted for most of his food. With his sleeker body, he could wade into deep water and still move quickly. Spinosaurus' quickness would be a big advantage in a fight.

SPINOSAURUS' WEAPONS

Spinosaurus had a long, flat snout like a crocodile. His long jaws were full of huge, deadly teeth. But unlike most **carnivores**, Spinosaurus had teeth that were spaced fairly far apart. They were straight, smooth, and cone-shaped. They were made for stabbing through meat rather than slicing it. Scientists think his teeth and jaws were made for catching fish instead of killing large **prey** on land.

FIERCE FACT
DESTROYED FOSSILS

The first Spinosaurus fossils ever discovered were destroyed in a bombing raid in Germany during World War II (1939–1945). No other Spinosaurus fossils were found until the 1980s.

Like many other predators, Spinosaurus had three clawed fingers on each hand. But while many large meat-eaters had very short arms, Spinosaurus' arms were much longer. He would have a big reach advantage against Giganotosaurus.

carnivore — an animal that eats only meat

prey — an animal that is hunted by other animals

GIGANOTOSAURUS' WEAPONS

At 8 inches (20 centimeters) long, Giganotosaurus' teeth were enormous. They were flat like a shark's teeth, but they were longer and narrower. They were **serrated** like a knife blade to slice through flesh and cause a lot of bleeding.

If Giganotosaurus got hold of his enemies, they were in trouble. Although he was a little smaller than Spinosaurus, his jaws were much more powerful. His superior bite strength would be a huge advantage in any fight.

serrated — having a jagged edge

14

The first Giganotosaurus skeleton was discovered in Argentina by an auto mechanic who hunted for fossils in his spare time.

Giganotosaurus also had sharp claws on each of his six fingers. He could use these curved claws for slashing an enemy or gripping his prey.

ATTACK STYLE

Spinosaurus
Nimble slasher

★ ★ ★ ★ ★

★ ★ ★ ★ ★

Giganotosaurus
Ferocious biter

Spinosaurus was built to hunt in the water and on land. Evidence shows that he ate fish and other dinosaurs. His long snout and unique teeth were made to grab and hang onto wildly squirming prey. With his long arms, he could stab at fish in the water or grab a victim on land. His neck was longer than the necks of most large meat-eaters. It allowed him to quickly dart his head forward to grab prey. In a fight, his long neck would provide a reach advantage against Giganotosaurus.

FIERCE FACT
THE SNOUT

Spinosaurus' nostrils sat fairly high on his snout. This feature allowed him to keep part of his snout underwater while still breathing.

Some scientists think Giganotosaurus hunted in packs. It might seem unnecessary for such a large predator, but hunting in packs would have helped bring down huge prey. Giganotosaurus probably hunted mighty **herbivores** like Argentinosaurus, which weighed nearly 100 tons (91 metric tons). A pack of Giganotosaurus probably bit their prey again and again. Each bite would tear away chunks of flesh until the victim bled to death.

herbivore — an animal that eats only plants

GET READY TO RUMBLE!

Are you ready for the main event? Two giant meat-eaters are out to prove who's the biggest, meanest beast of the prehistoric world. In one corner is the fierce hunter — Spinosaurus! He's big, he's tough, and he's mean. In the other corner is his opponent — Giganotosaurus! His name says it all. He's gigantic, deadly, and hungry. Nobody can guess which of these super-sized dinosaurs will win this fight. But one thing is certain — the winner will be bloody, battered, and bruised!

You've got a front row seat. So grab your favorite snack and drink, turn the page, and get ready to enjoy the battle!

SPINOSAURUS

★ ★ ★ ★ ★
SIZE

★ ★ ★
SPEED AND AGILITY
★ ★

★ ★ ★ ★
WEAPONS
★ ★ ★ ★

★ ★ ★ ★ ★
ATTACK STYLE
★ ★ ★ ★ ★

GIGANOTOSAURUS

ONE LAST THING...

This battle is make-believe. Like Goldilocks and the three bears — it never happened. Even scientists don't know everything about these two mighty dinosaurs. But we know they were big, mean, and hungry — and they could fight. This should be one gigantic good show!

PAIN

Spinosaurus splashes through the ocean. He cranes his neck low and scans the water. Just beyond him, stormy waves crash down. Foamy water rumbles toward the shore. Neither the rain nor the violent sea seems to bother the monstrous Spinosaurus.

Suddenly, he plunges his long snout into the salty water. His jaws snap shut. Below the surface, his teeth bite into the tail of a long, brown fish. He jerks his snout upward to pull the fish from the water. The fish thrashes wildly and begins to slip from his grasp.

The hungry beast clamps his mouth tight to get a better grip. But the fish slips and splashes into the sea. Spinosaurus swipes his clawed hand through the water to grab the big fish. Then he flips it into the air and catches it in his toothy jaws.

He holds the struggling fish tightly in his jaws and turns toward the shore. There he sees Giganotosaurus.

Fossils show that some fish living at the time of Spinosaurus grew up to 20 feet (6 meters) long. These fish would have made a decent meal for even the largest Spinosaurus.

FIERCE FACT
BIG MEAL

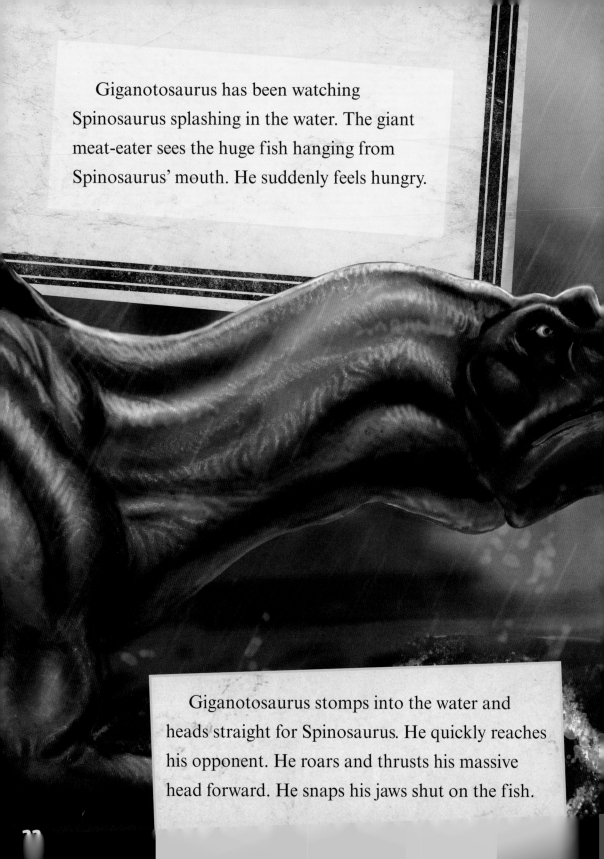

Giganotosaurus has been watching Spinosaurus splashing in the water. The giant meat-eater sees the huge fish hanging from Spinosaurus' mouth. He suddenly feels hungry.

Giganotosaurus stomps into the water and heads straight for Spinosaurus. He quickly reaches his opponent. He roars and thrusts his massive head forward. He snaps his jaws shut on the fish.

Spinosaurus tries to jerk the fish away, but Giganotosaurus holds on tightly. The two giant predators tug again. Suddenly, the fish breaks apart. Giganotosaurus stumbles deeper into the water. He's already off balance when a towering wave slams into him. He plunges into the dark sea.

Giganotosaurus means "giant southern lizard."

FIERCE FACT

NAME

Giganotosaurus crashes into the wet sand beneath the water. He lifts his head and climbs to his feet. But Spinosaurus is waiting for him. He snaps his long jaws around Giganotosaurus' neck.

Giganotosaurus roars. Spinosaurus holds on tight. He tugs his opponent farther into the water. Giganotosaurus stumbles and falls to his knees. Spinosaurus forces his enemy's head below the dark waves. He leans his massive body weight against his foe to hold him under the water.

Giganotosaurus tries to roar. But his mouth fills with salty water. He begins to panic. He finds the sandy bottom with his feet and pushes up with all his strength. He rises wildly out of the foamy water. But Spinosaurus is still gripping his neck. The two giant dinosaurs topple sideways and crash into the stormy sea.

Spinosaurus means "spine lizard."

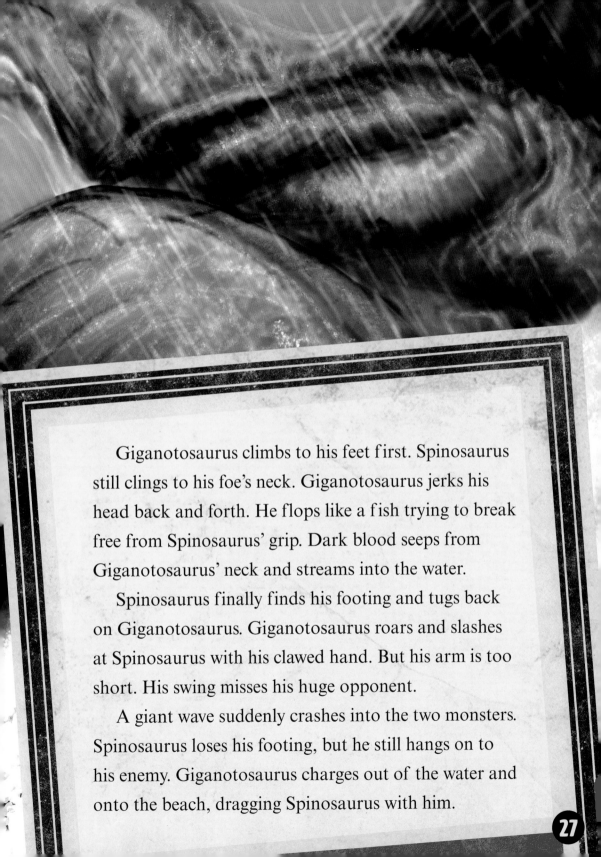

Giganotosaurus climbs to his feet first. Spinosaurus still clings to his foe's neck. Giganotosaurus jerks his head back and forth. He flops like a fish trying to break free from Spinosaurus' grip. Dark blood seeps from Giganotosaurus' neck and streams into the water.

Spinosaurus finally finds his footing and tugs back on Giganotosaurus. Giganotosaurus roars and slashes at Spinosaurus with his clawed hand. But his arm is too short. His swing misses his huge opponent.

A giant wave suddenly crashes into the two monsters. Spinosaurus loses his footing, but he still hangs on to his enemy. Giganotosaurus charges out of the water and onto the beach, dragging Spinosaurus with him.

Spinosaurus' weight causes Giganotosaurus to stumble. He falls and crashes hard on top of his enemy. Spinosaurus finally loses his grip on Giganotosaurus' neck. Both dinosaurs struggle to climb to their feet.

Spinosaurus rises first. He opens his jaws wide. He darts his head forward to strike. But Giganotosaurus ducks out of the way. He springs forward and clamps his powerful jaws onto Spinosaurus' neck. Spinosaurus shrieks and tries to pull away.

Giganotosaurus twists violently with his powerful neck muscles and massive body. There's a loud snap! Giganotosaurus lets go of Spinosaurus' neck. Spinosaurus flops to the ground. The battle is over.

Giganotosaurus stomps powerfully in the wet sand. He points his huge head toward the stormy sky and bellows a mighty roar. He lets the world know he's just beaten one of the biggest predators ever to walk the earth!

GLOSSARY

carnivore (KAHR-nuh-vor) — an animal that eats only meat

extinct (ik-STINGKT) — no longer living; an extinct animal is one whose kind has died out completely.

fossil (FAH-suhl) — the remains or traces of plants and animals that are preserved as rock

herbivore (HUR-buh-vor) — an animal that eats only plants

nostril (NOS-truhl) — an opening in an animal's nose through which it breathes and smells

predator (PRED-uh-tur) — an animal that hunts other animals for food

prey (PRAY) — an animal hunted by another animal for food

serrated (SER-ay-tid) — having a jagged edge that helps with cutting, such as a saw

stocky (STOK-ee) — having a strong, heavy build

READ MORE

Kelley, K. C. *Deadly Dinos*. Boys Rock!
Chanhassen, Minn.: Child's World, 2006.

Shone, Rob. *Giganotosaurus: The Giant
Southern Lizard*. Graphic Dinosaurs.
New York: Rosen, 2009.

Thomson, Sarah L. *Extreme Dinosaurs!
Q & A*. Smithsonian Q & A. New York:
Collins, 2007.

INTERNET SITES

FactHound offers a safe, fun way to find Internet
sites related to this book. All of the sites on
FactHound have been researched by our staff.

Here's all you do:

Visit *www.facthound.com*

FactHound will fetch the best sites for you!

INDEX

DATE DUE

NV 15 '11			
MR 2 5 '11			
MT 2 1 2			
			Demco